Pebble®

How Fruits and Vegetables Grow

Blueberries
Grow on a Bush

by Mari Schuh

Consulting Editor: Gail Saunders-Smith, PhD

Consultant: Sarah Pounders, education specialist
National Gardening Association

CAPSTONE PRESS
a capstone imprint

Pebble Books are published by Capstone Press,
151 Good Counsel Drive, P.O. Box 669, Mankato, Minnesota 56002.
www.capstonepub.com

Books published by Capstone Press are manufactured with paper
containing at least 10 percent post-consumer waste.

Library of Congress Cataloging-in-Publication Data
Schuh, Mari C., 1975–
  Blueberries grow on a bush / by Mari Schuh.
    p. cm.—(Pebble books. How fruits and vegetables grow)
  Summary: "Simple text and photographs describe how blueberries grow on
bushes"—Provided by publisher.
  Includes bibliographical references and index.
  ISBN 978-1-4296-5282-7 (library binding)
  ISBN 978-1-4296-6183-6 (paperback)
  1. Blueberries—Juvenile literature. I. Title. II. Series: Pebble (Mankato, Minn.).
How fruits and vegetables grow.
  SB386.B7S65 2011
  634′.737—dc22
                                                                    2010025470

Note to Parents and Teachers

The How Fruits and Vegetables Grow set supports national science
standards related to life science. This book describes and illustrates
how blueberries grow on bushes. The images support early readers
in understanding the text. The repetition of words and phrases helps
early readers learn new words. This book also introduces early
readers to subject-specific vocabulary words, which are defined in
the Glossary section. Early readers may need assistance to read some
words and to use the Table of Contents, Glossary, Read More, Internet
Sites, and Index sections of the book.

Printed in the United States of America in North Mankato, Minnesota.
092010
005933CGS11

Table of Contents

4

Bursting with Berries

Round bushes grow
in the bright sun.
The bushes are full
of juicy berries.

seeds

bushes

Life Cycle of a Blueberry Bush

flowers

blueberries

6

Growing

Many kinds of bushes
make berries. The berries
grow in similar ways.
Blueberries are one kind
of fruit from bushes.

fruit

leaves

branch

Blueberries need lots
of sun to grow.
Blueberry bushes grow
best in moist, acidic soil.

In spring, blueberry bushes grow green leaves.
White or pink flowers cover the bushes. The flowers are shaped like bells.

Pollination

Bees pollinate the flowers.
Now the flowers are
fertilized and make seeds.
Each flower makes one
blueberry to hold the seeds.

Ripening and Resting

Clusters of blueberries grow
on the bushes. The berries
ripen at different times.
Blueberries are picked
in spring, summer, and fall.

16

The cold winter comes.
Most bushes lose
their leaves. They rest to get
ready for spring. This time
of rest is called dormancy.

blackberries

raspberries

huckleberries

Bushes Grow Many Berries

Different bushes grow different berries. People pick blackberries, raspberries, and huckleberries off bushes.

gooseberries

black currants

red currants

Gooseberries and black
and red currants also grow
on bushes. Bushes give us
plenty of healthy fruit to eat.

Glossary

acidic soil—a type of soil that is made up of chemicals in certain amounts; some plants grow better in acidic soil

cluster—a group of objects that are close together; most blueberries grow in clusters

dormancy—a time of rest; many kinds of bushes and trees are dormant during winter

fertilize—to start seed growth in a plant

moist—slightly wet

pollinate—to move tiny yellow grains called pollen from flower to flower; pollination lets plants and flowers make seeds

ripen—to become ready to be harvested, picked, or eaten

Read More

Bodach, Vijaya Khisty. *Fruits.* Plant Parts. Mankato, Minn.: Capstone Press, 2007.

Schuh, Mari. *Growing a Garden.* Gardens. Mankato, Minn.: Capstone Press, 2010.

Spilsbury, Louise. *Fruits.* Eat Smart. Chicago: Heinemann Library, 2009.

Internet Sites

FactHound offers a safe, fun way to find Internet sites related to this book. All of the sites on FactHound have been researched by our staff.

Here's all you do:

Visit *www.facthound.com*

Type in this code: 9781429652827

Check out projects, games and lots more at
www.capstonekids.com

Index

Word Count: 166
Grade: 1
Early-Intervention Level: 21

Editorial Credits
Erika L. Shores, editor; Bobbie Nuytten, designer; Wanda Winch, media researcher;
Laura Manthe, production specialist

Photo Credits
Capstone Press: Karon Dubke, 6 (top left); iStockphoto: 2ndLookGraphics, 12
(bottom left), Carmen Reed, 6 (top right), Karen Massier, 16; Shutterstock: alexwhite,
cover (green leaf element), Beata Becia, cover, (blueberry element throughout book),
Domrose Hub-With, 20 (bottom), Ingor Normann, 18 (top), Jason Vandehey, 4, Jeff
Strickler, 14, newa, 18 (bottom), SunnyS, 12, Thomas Pavelka, 20 (top), Travis Manley,
6 (bottom), 8, vahamrick, 6 (middle), 10, Vladimir Konjushenko, 20 (middle),
Vphoto, 18 (middle)

**The author dedicates this book to the memory of her beloved pet rabbit, Karma,
who will forever be begging for blueberries.**